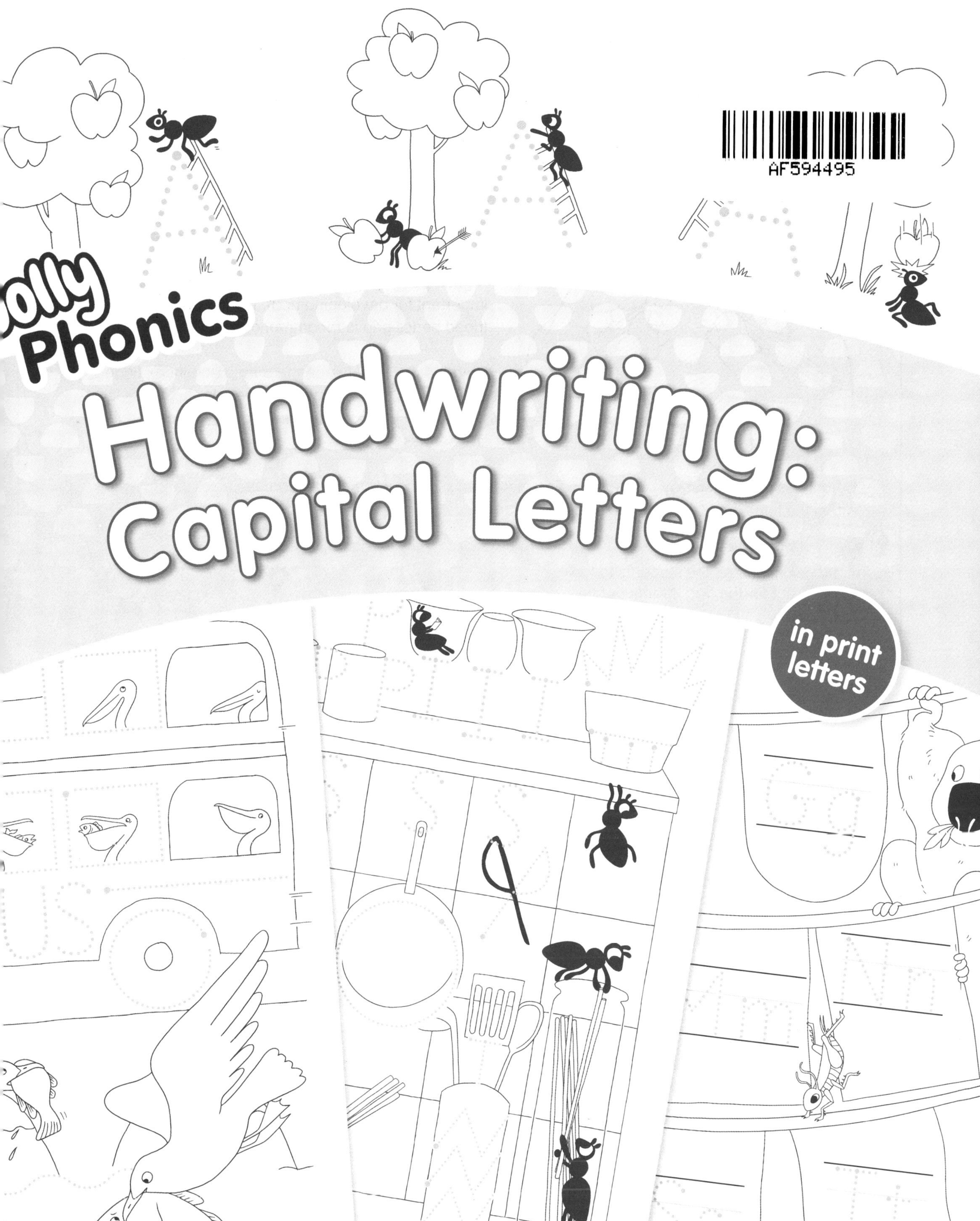

Ideal for developing good pencil control and correct formation

Guidelines

Good pencil control and correct formation (including knowing how to start and finish each letter) enable students to achieve neat, fluent and, eventually, joined handwriting.

Handwriting practice works best when the students are sitting at their table or desk. This provides a firm, flat surface to write on and encourages correct posture.

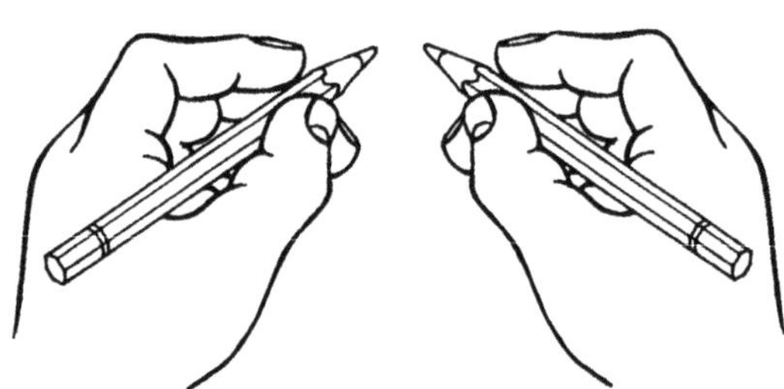

A good pencil grip from the very beginning is extremely important for developing neat, fluent handwriting. The tripod pencil grip is recommended.

Hold the pencil between the thumb and index finger, and support it on the middle finger. As the pencil is moved, the knuckles on the thumb and index finger look like a frog's legs.

Coloring is also a good way to develop fine motor skills. Encourage the students to color carefully, to keep within the lines, and to choose appropriate colors.

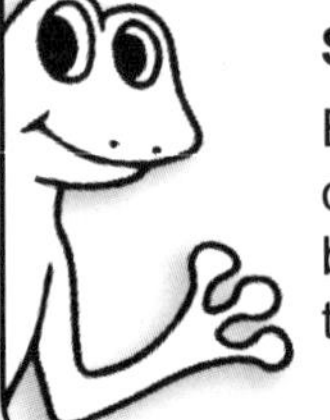

Spot the frog

Encourage the students to look out for the frog throughout this book, to remind them to practice their "froggy-leg" grip.

Icon key

Draw/trace the lines/color

Talk about the picture

Look closer

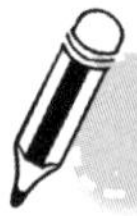

Write your name in the flag and complete the castle.

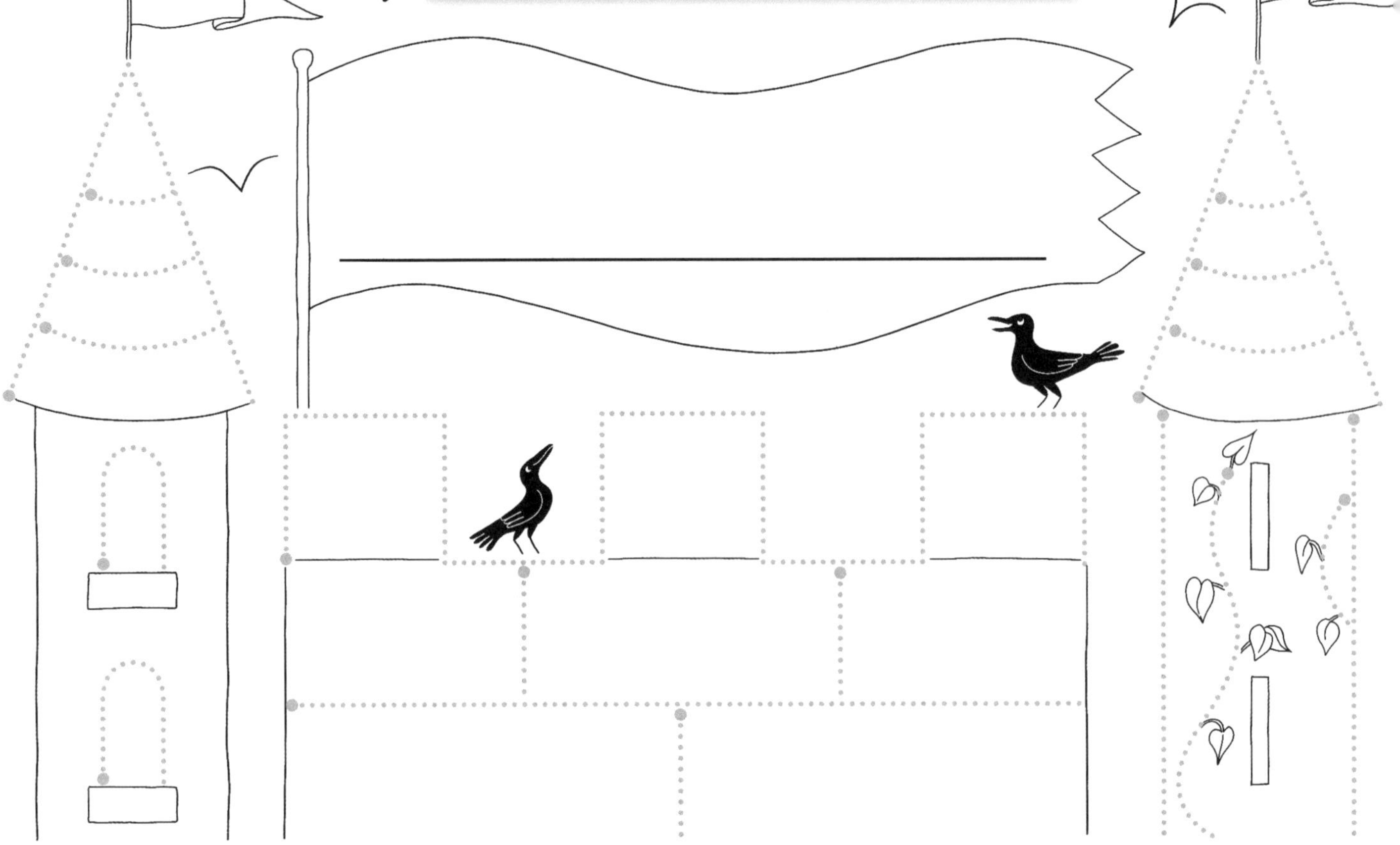

s S

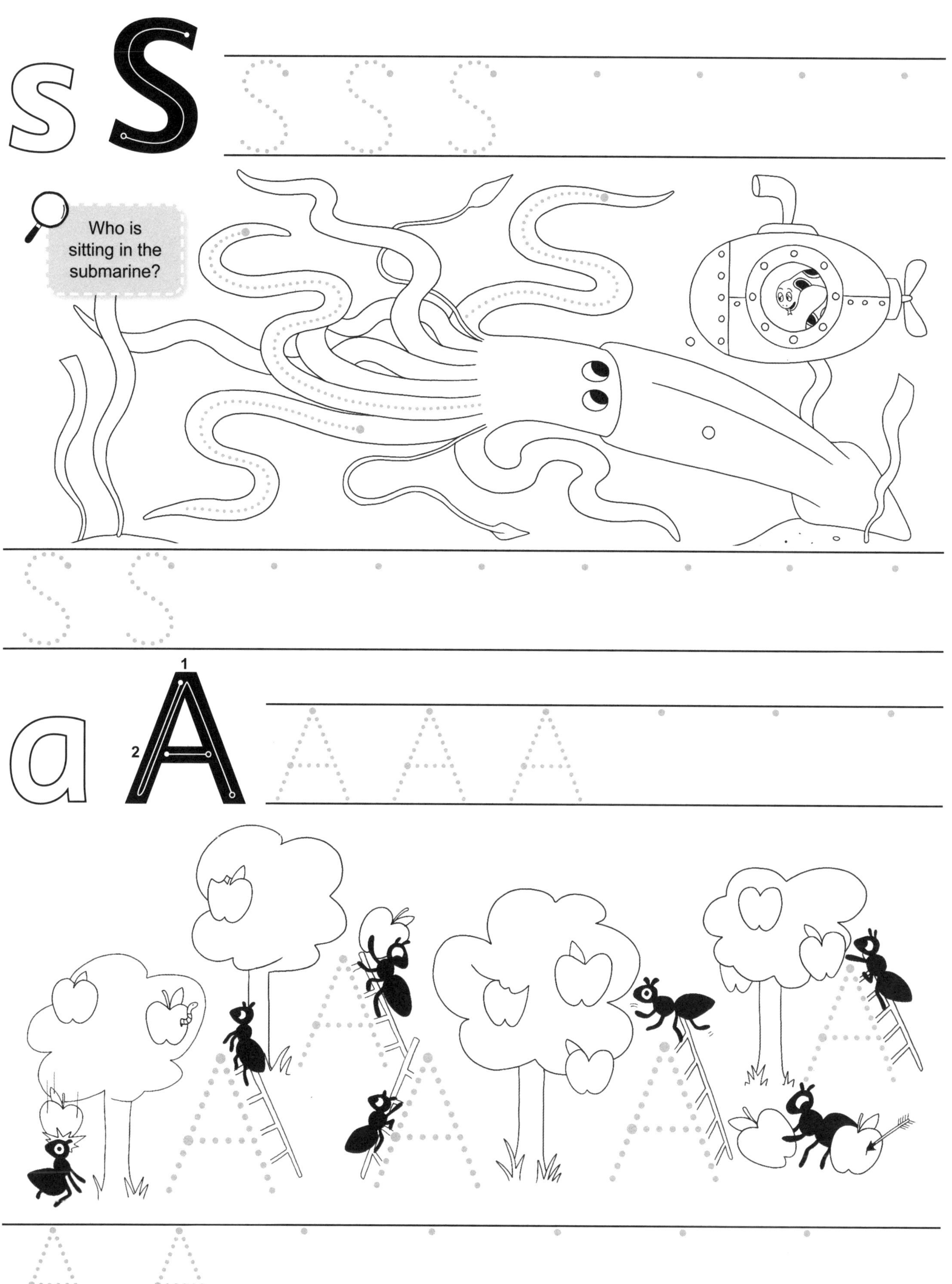

a A

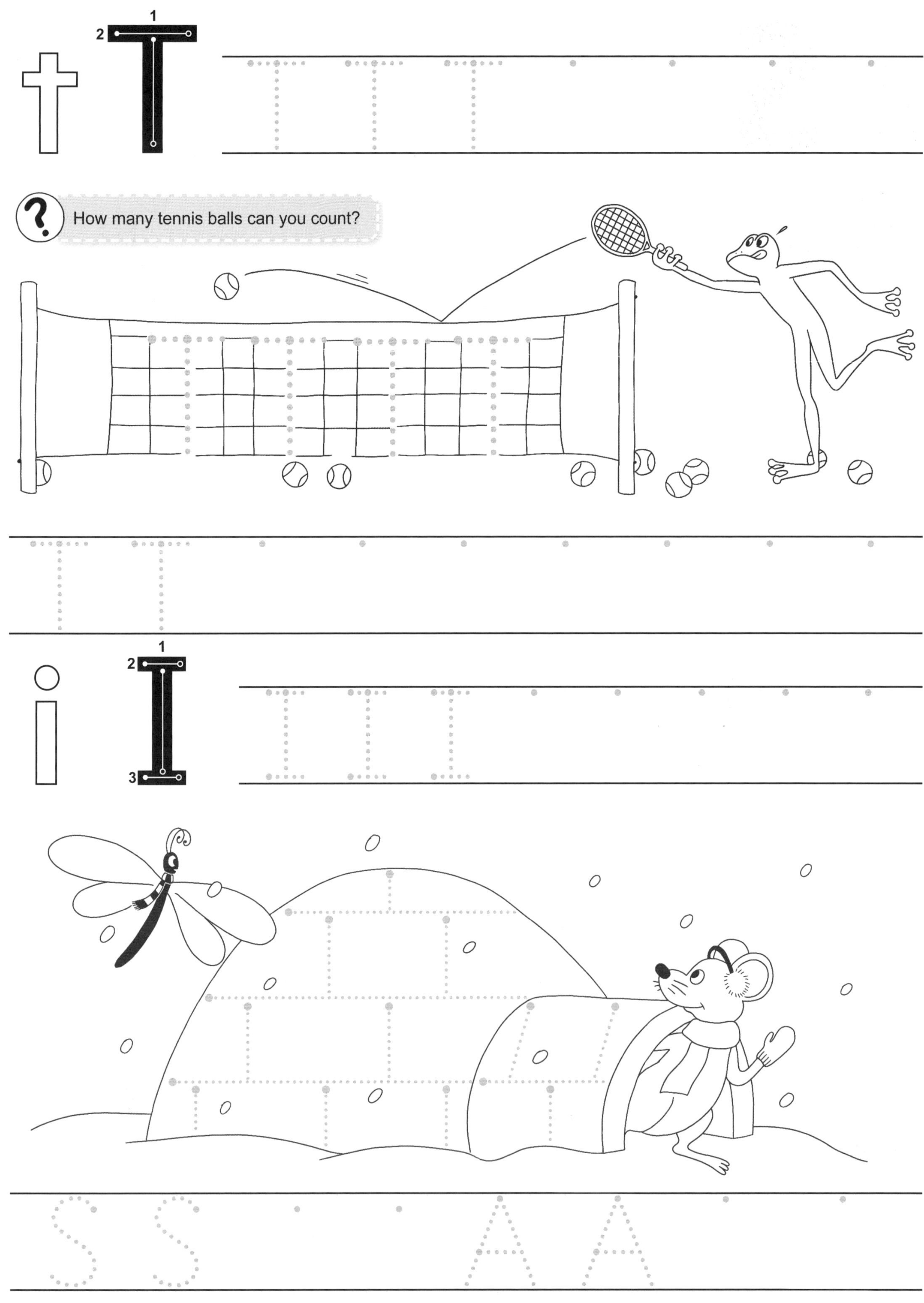
1
2
How many tennis balls can you count?
1
2
3

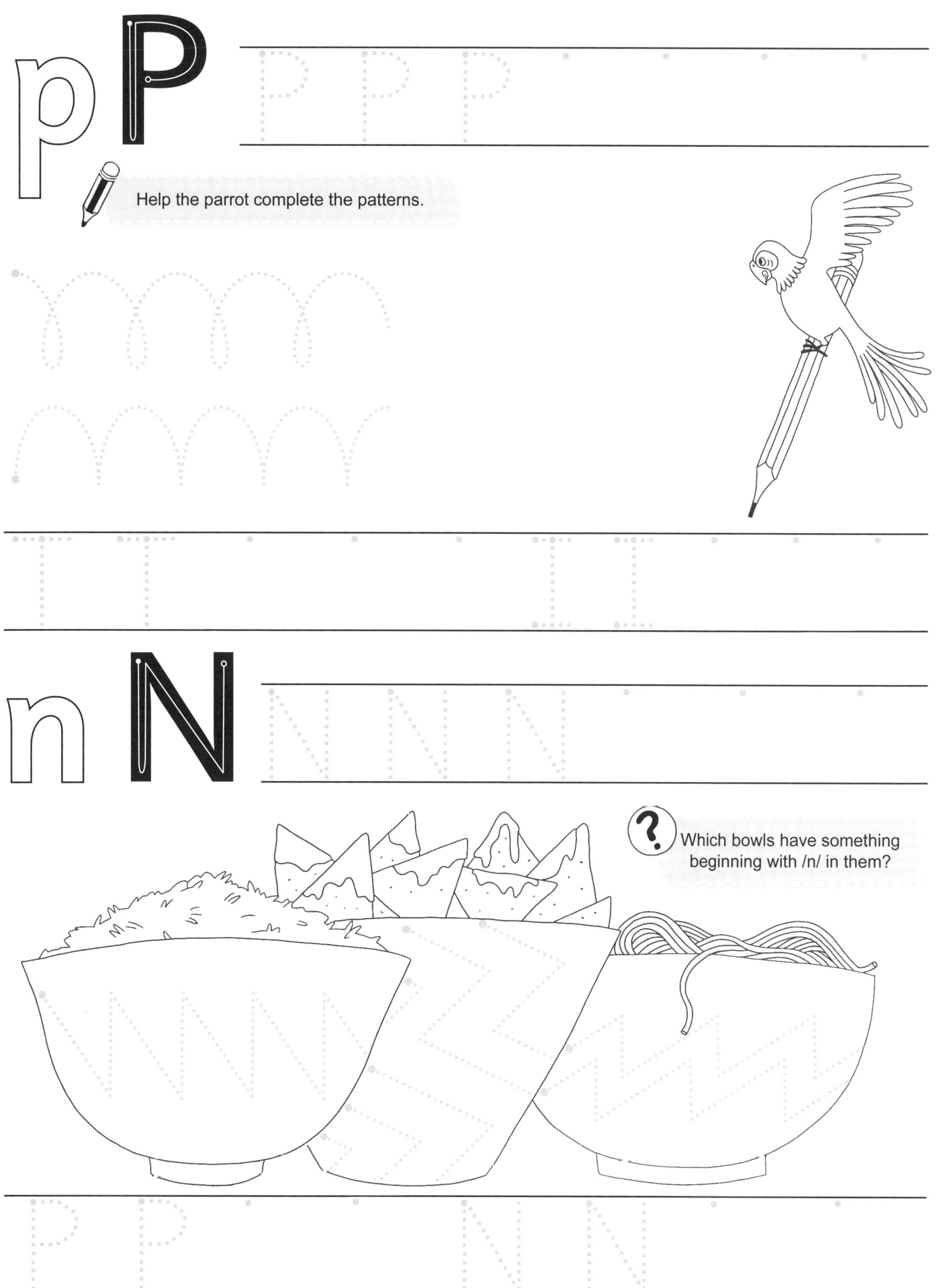

p P
Help the parrot complete the patterns.
n N
Which bowls have something beginning with /n/ in them?

Ants sit in a pan.

Ants snip pasta.

Find out which envelope goes to which door by matching the capital and lower-case letters.

S S S

N N N

I I I

T T T

P P P

A A A

t n p a s i

c C
Can you walk like a crab and click your claws like castanets?
1
2
k K

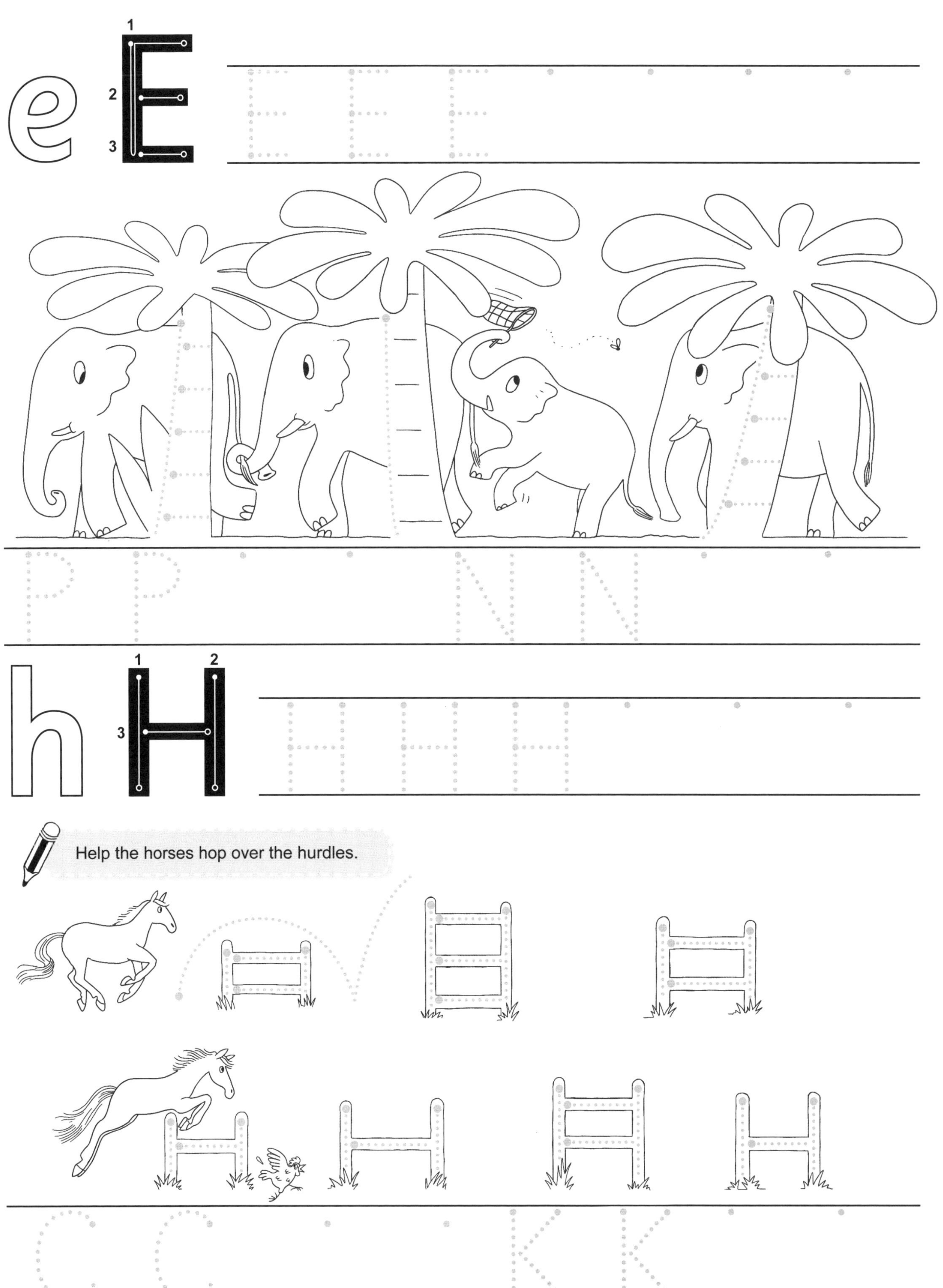
e E
1
2
3
h H
1
2
3
Help the horses hop over the hurdles.

r R

m M

d D

Crickets did

handstands.

Match the capital and lower-case letters to see which firework comes from which box.

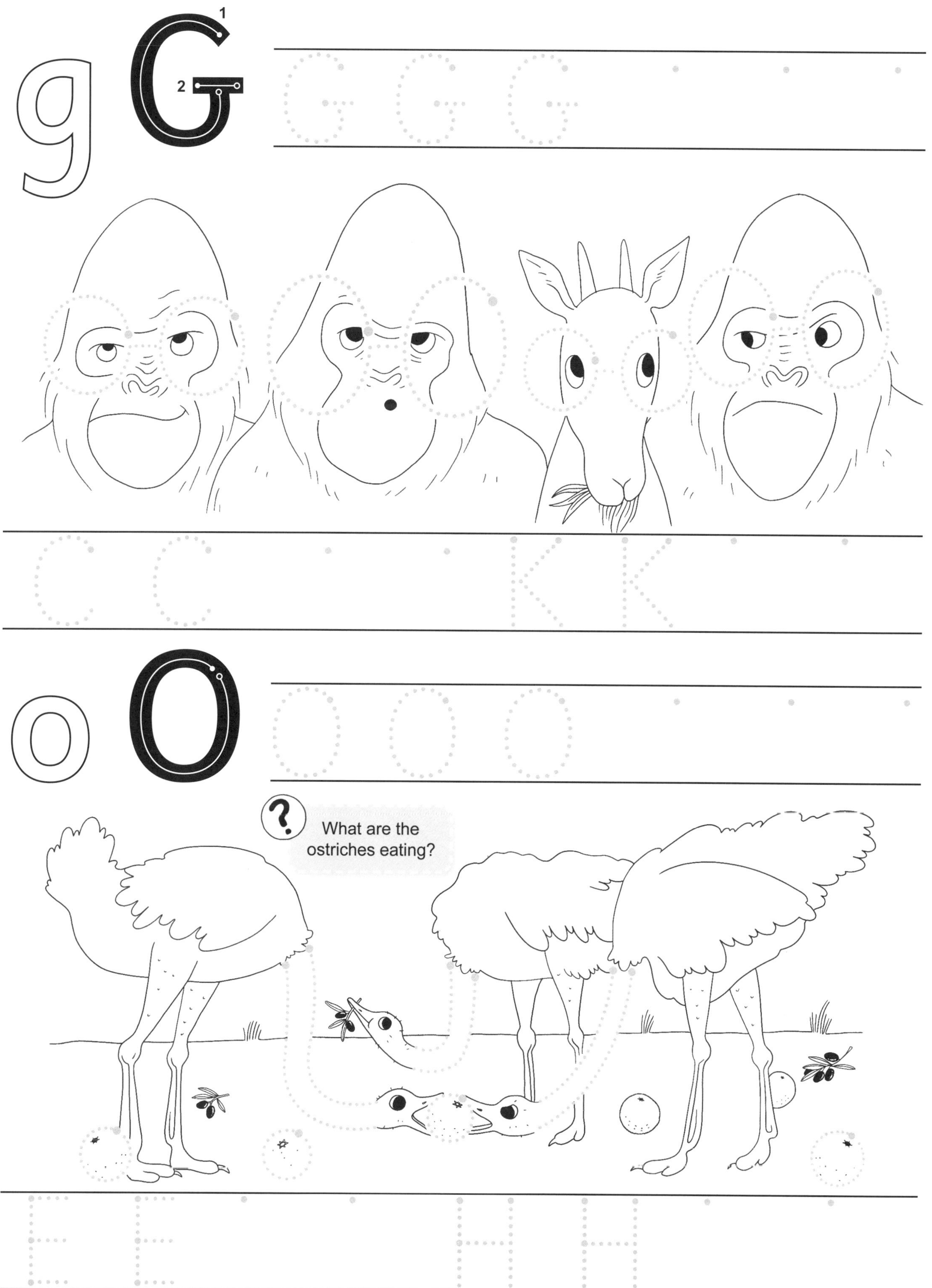
What are the ostriches eating?

u U

l L

f F
1
2
Draw something beginning with the /f/ sound on each flag.
b B
Which of these foods start with a /b/?

Ten pelicans sit on a bus.
BUS
Gulls grab cod.

Find out which rocket is going to which planet by matching the capital and lower-case letters.

j J
z Z
How many of your clothes have zippers on them?

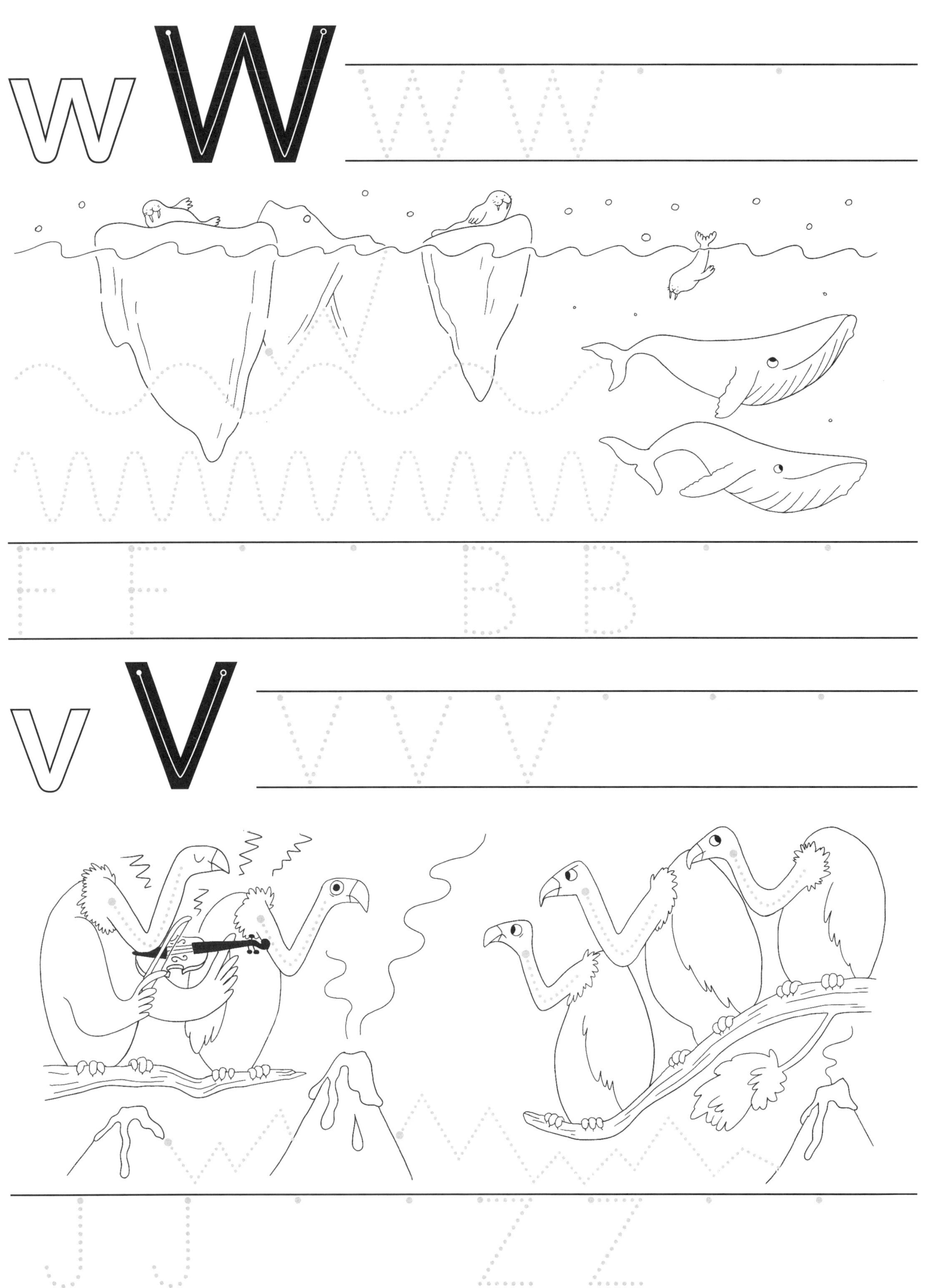

y Y
1
2
x X
1
2
Help the fox fix the rug.
How many foxes can you count?

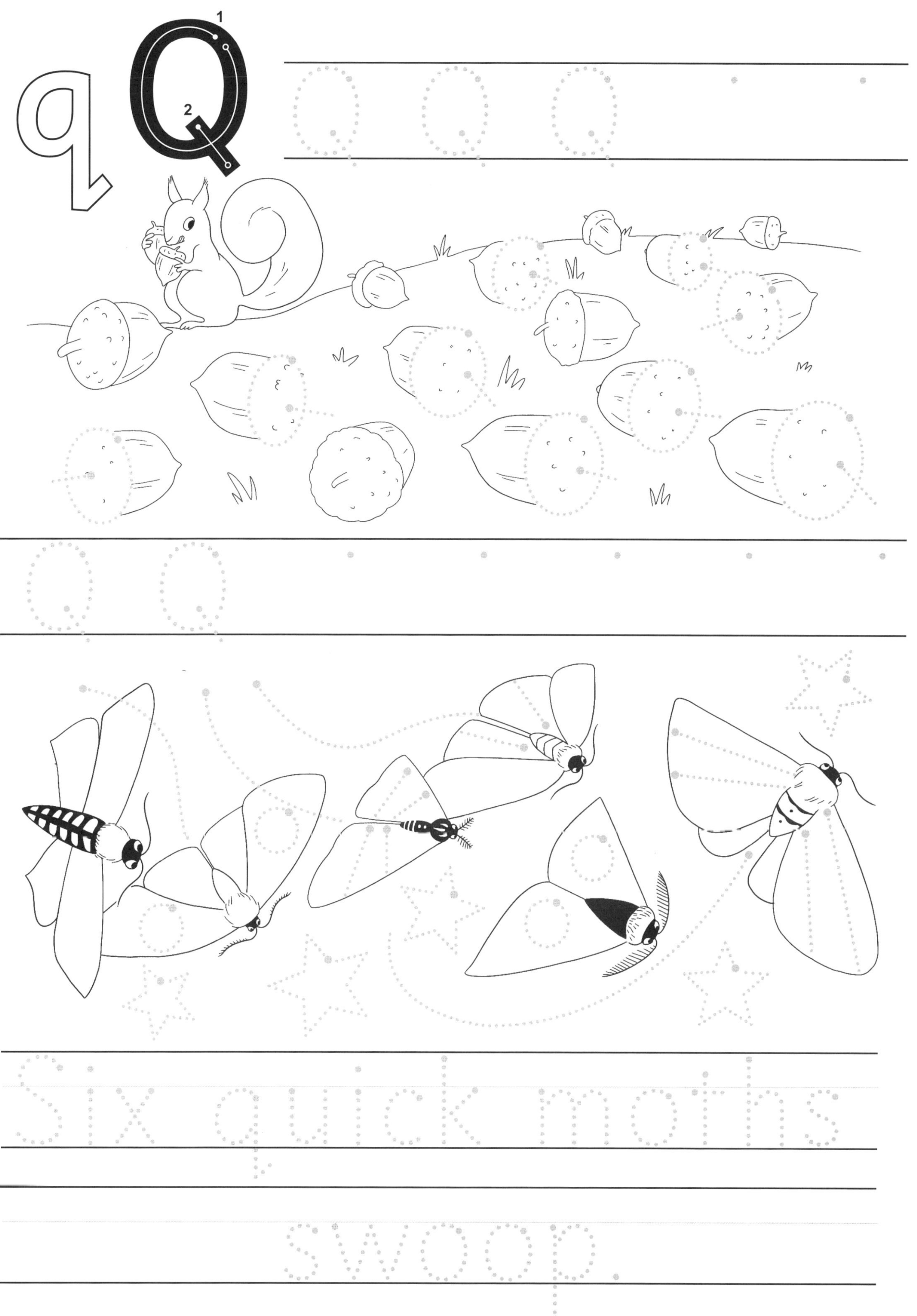
q Q
1
2
Six quick moths
swoop.

Fill in the letters of the alphabet.

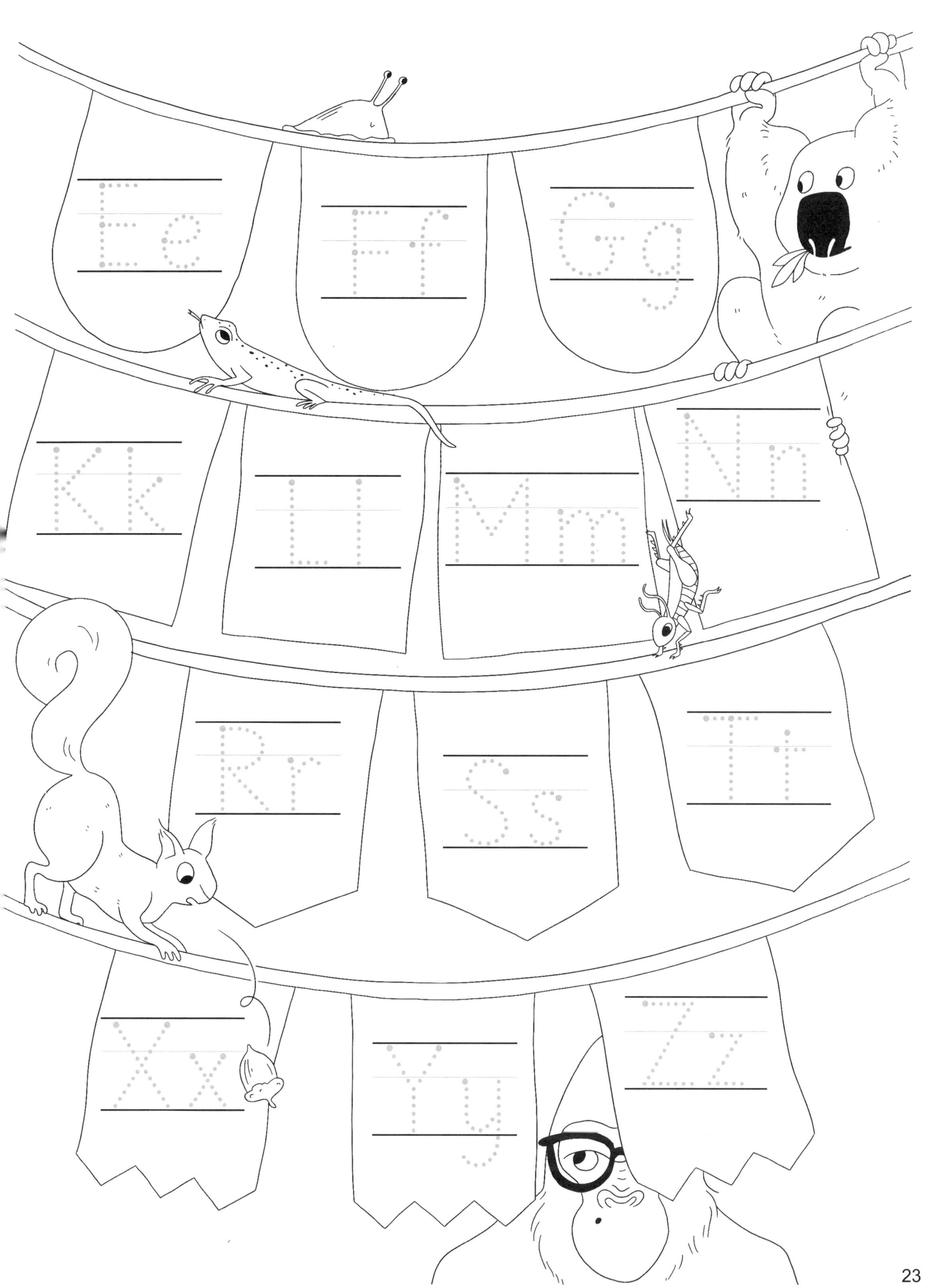
Ee
Ff
Gg
Kk
Ll
Mm
Nn
Rr
Ss
Tt
Xx
Yy
Zz

Ages 4+

Jolly Phonics Handwriting: Capital Letters

Perfect for practicing capital letter formation

This book provides capital letter formation practice for beginner writers. It focuses on the capital letters taught in Step 2 and includes upper- and lower-case matching activities to reinforce the link between the capitals and their letter sounds. Dotted letters and words (with starting dots) remind students how the letters are formed, and encourage them to write words using the letter sounds they know. Each page features fun activities to complete and attractive pictures to color, which help the students to develop fine motor control.

Other books in the series:

Seven books covering the letter-sound groups taught in Step 1.

Jolly Phonics — **To see the full range of Jolly Phonics products, visit our website at www.jollylearning.com**

82 Winter Sport Lane, Williston,
VT 05495, USA. Tel: +1-800-488-2665
77 Hornbeam Road, Buckhurst Hill, Essex,
IG9 6JX, UK. Tel: +44 20 8501 0405

www.jollylearning.com info@jollylearning.co.uk

ISBN 978-1-83582-276-0

Reference: JL2760